DEDICATION

This book is dedicated to my youngest son, Khatari, and to my mother, Theresa McCalley, who shaped my identity by never letting me forget who I am as an Afrikan descendant, and who taught me to value every glorious aspect of Afrikan identity, culture, and heritage.

No Fruits Without The Roots

Before the blossom, before the seed,
Before young hands could learn to read,
Before the fruit hung bright and proud,
There was soil beneath the crowd.

Hidden deep where eyes can't see,
History feeds the growing tree.
Struggles buried, tears like rain,
Sunlight rising after pain.

From broken chains and muted cries,
From stubborn hope that would not die,
From fields once scarred by unjust hands,
Came roots that learned to understand.

They twisted strong through rock and doubt,
They held the shifting earth in place,
They drank from truth, refused to bow,
They built tomorrow out of now.

Beneath each ring of living wood
Lives all the things misunderstood.
The cost. The courage. Quiet proof.
The strength that settles in the root.

So when the branches stretch up high,
And leaves grow bold against the sky,
Remember what the surface hides —
The unseen force that still abides.

For greatness never falls like rain,
It rises slowly through the strain.
And in the quiet earth beneath the suits,

a tree is only as strong as its roots.

CARTER G. WOODSON

BEFORE TRUTH FILLED THE CLASSROOM PAGE,
BEFORE OUR NAMES STOOD ON THE STAGE,
THERE WAS A MAN WHO SAW THE COST
OF HISTORY HIDDEN, TWISTED, LOST.
HE NOTICED BOOKS THAT TOLD ONE SIDE,
WHILE OTHER VOICES HAD TO HIDE.
HE KNEW WHEN STORIES DISAPPEAR,
A PEOPLE'S FUTURE ISN'T CLEAR.
SO CARTER READ.
AND CARTER WROTE.
HE TURNED FORGOTTEN FACTS TO HOPE.
HE CARVED A WEEK INTO THE YEAR
SO BLACK HISTORY WOULD REAPPEAR.
THAT WEEK GREW STRONG — IT DID NOT BEND.
IT GREW INTO A MONTH WE NOW DEFEND.
HE TAUGHT US THIS, BOTH PROUD AND TRUE:
TO KNOW YOUR ROOTS IS POWER IN YOU.

Short Bio

Dr. Carter G. Woodson (1875–1950) was a historian, educator, and author who believed people must know their true history to understand themselves. In 1926, he created Negro History Week, which later became Black History Month. His book The Miseducation of the Negro challenged how history was taught and encouraged critical thinking about identity and education. He dedicated his life to preserving Black history so future generations would know their roots.

HISTORY
2+2=4
1+1=2
LIL' CARTER

HEUY P. NEWTON

Short Bio

Huey P. Newton was a revolutionary thinker and co-founder of the Black Panther Party. He believed education, self-respect, and community care were essential tools for freedom. Huey encouraged people to study history, protect one another, and never accept injustice as normal.

LIL' HUEY

ASSATA SHAKUR

ASSATA SHAKUR WALKED SILENT BUT STRONG,
WITH LOVE FOR THE PEOPLE ALL HER LIFE LONG.
SHE STOOD FIRM FOR JUSTICE, BRAVE WITHOUT FEAR,
FACING DOWN WRONG — LIBERATION CAME NEAR.
WHEN ROADS WERE HARD AND JOURNEYS LONG,
HER SPIRIT STAYED ROOTED, BRAVE AND STRONG.
SHE SHOWED US THAT TRUTH, WITH HEART AND MIND,
IS A GIFT WE CARRY FOR ALL HUMANKIND.

Short Bio

Assata Shakur was a courageous freedom fighter who stood up for justice and dignity. She believed in liberation, community love, and truth. Her strength and compassion continue to inspire people around the world.

Lil' Asaata

FRED HAMPTON

FRED HAMPTON SPOKE WITH PRIDE,
NEVER BREAKING HIS STRIDE.
WITH LOVE FOR THE PEOPLE DEEP INSIDE,
HE STOOD UP TALL, THOUGH HE WAS YOUNG,
TEACHING UNITY — FIRE FROM HIS TONGUE.
HE BUILT A RAINBOW COALITION STRONG,
SAYING JUSTICE BELONGS TO ALL, NOT SOME.
HE FED THE CHILDREN, HE SERVED THE POOR,
KNOCKING FEARLESSLY ON FREEDOM'S DOOR.
WITH COURAGE SHINING LIKE A STAR IN THE SKY,
HE SHOWED US HOW TO STAND WITH OUR HEADS HELD
HIGH.

Short Bio
Fred Hampton (1948–1969) was chairman of the Illinois chapter
of the Black Panther Party. He organized free breakfast programs
for children and built the Rainbow Coalition, uniting different
communities to fight injustice together. Though only 21 years old
when he fell, his message of unity and courage continues
to inspire generations

LIL' FRED

ROSA PARKS

ROSA PARKS SAT CALM AND STILL,
WITH QUIET STRENGTH AND IRON WILL.
WHEN TOLD TO MOVE AND GIVE HER SEAT,
SHE CHOSE TO STAND BY STAYING IN HER SEAT.
NOT LOUD, NOT WILD, NOT FILLED WITH RAGE,
BUT BRAVE ENOUGH TO CHANGE AN AGE.
ON A BUS ONE DAY IN ALABAMA TOWN,
SHE WOULD NOT LET INJUSTICE PUSH HER DOWN.
HER "NO" WAS SOFT — BUT STRONG AND CLEAR,
A WHISPER THE WHOLE WORLD COULD HEAR.
SHE SHOWED US COURAGE DOESN'T SHOUT,
SOMETIMES IT'S WHAT YOU WON'T DO THAT COUNTS.

Short Bio

Rosa Parks was a civil rights activist who helped spark the Montgomery Bus Boycott in 1955 after refusing to give up her seat to a white passenger in Alabama. Her peaceful act of resistance became a powerful symbol in the fight against segregation and unjust Jim Crow laws in the South. She worked alongside leaders like Dr. Martin Luther King Jr. and remained active in the movement for justice her entire life.

Lil' Rosa

HARRIET TUBMAN

HARRIET TUBMAN WAS BRAVE AND STRONG,
SHE KNEW RIGHT FROM WRONG HER WHOLE LIFE LONG.
SHE COULD'VE BEEN FREE AND STAYED AWAY,
BUT HER SPIRIT SAID, "GO BACK—LEAD THE WAY."
THROUGH DARK OF NIGHT AND PATHS UNKNOWN,
SHE WALKED WITH COURAGE ALL HER OWN.
THE UNDERGROUND RAILROAD WAS HER FIGHT,
GUIDING OTHERS TOWARD FREEDOM'S LIGHT.
SHE FEARED NO DANGER, SHE FEARED NO MAN,
SHE MOVED WITH WISDOM, HEART, AND PLAN.
A WARRIOR WOMAN, STEADY AND TRUE,
SHE NEVER QUIT—SHE ALWAYS CAME THROUGH.
HARRIET FOUGHT SO OTHERS COULD SEE,
THAT FREEDOM BELONGS TO YOU AND ME.
A LITTLE LEGEND, FIERCE AND WISE,
WITH FREEDOM'S FIRE IN HER EYES.

Short Bio

Harriet Tubman was a freedom fighter who led many people to safety through the Underground Railroad. She could have stayed free, but she returned again and again because she cared for others. Her life teaches us courage, wisdom, and love for the people.

Lil' Harriet

MARTIN LUTHER KING, JR.

MARTIN KING DREAMED BIG AND SPOKE OUT LOUD,
HE STOOD FOR JUSTICE, CALM AND PROUD.
HE BELIEVED THAT LOVE COULD LEAD THE WAY,
AND CHANGE THE WORLD DAY BY DAY.
WITH PEACEFUL WORDS AND FEARLESS HEART,
HE KNEW THAT TRUTH IS WHERE WE START.
HE MARCHED, HE TAUGHT, HE STOOD UP STRONG,
SHOWING RIGHT CAN FIX WHAT'S WRONG.
HE SAID ALL PEOPLE SHOULD BE FREE,
TREATED WITH CARE AND DIGNITY.
WITH COURAGE, HOPE, AND STEADY HAND,
HE HELPED TO CHANGE THIS VERY LAND.
MARTIN KING REMINDS US ALL,
LOVE IS THE STRONGEST POWER OF ALL.

Short Bio

Martin Luther King Jr. was a leader who fought for civil rights using peace and love. He believed that nonviolence and unity could change unfair laws and hearts. His life teaches us to be brave, kind, and to stand up for what is right

LIL' MARTIN

MARCUS GARVEY

MARCUS GARVEY DREAMED OF A PEOPLE STRONG,
WHO KNEW THEIR ROOTS AND WHERE THEY BELONG.
HE TAUGHT AFRICAN DESCENDANT CHILDREN FAR AND WIDE,
TO WALK WITH TRUTH AND CARRY PRIDE.
HE WAVED A FLAG OF RED, BLACK, GREEN,
FOR BLOOD, FOR PEOPLE, FOR LANDS UNSEEN.
RED FOR STRENGTH AND ALL WE'VE BEEN THROUGH,
BLACK FOR THE PEOPLE — ME AND YOU.
GREEN FOR THE FUTURE, THE LAND, THE SEED,
A GROWING WORLD OUR CHILDREN NEED.
HE SAID, "KNOW SELF, STAND TALL, BE FREE,
A MIGHTY NATION YOU CAN BE."
LITTLE MARCUS SHOWS US TODAY,
OUR ROOTS GIVE POWER ALONG THE WAY.

Short Bio

Marcus Garvey was a Pan-African leader who believed African people everywhere should unite. He introduced the red, black, and green flag to African descendants in North America and taught pride, self-reliance, and self-determination. His message reminds us that knowing who we are makes us strong.

LIL' MARCUS

MALCOLM X

MALCOLM X STOOD SHARP AND WISE,
WITH TRUTH AND FIRE IN HIS EYES.
HE SPOKE FOR PEOPLE PUSHED ASIDE,
TEACHING STRENGTH AND INNER PRIDE.
HE STUDIED HISTORY, LAW, AND SELF,
SAID FREEDOM STARTS WITH KNOWING YOURSELF.
NO LIES, NO FEAR, NO BENDING LOW,
HE TAUGHT THE PEOPLE HOW TO GROW.
HE CHANGED, HE LEARNED, HE STAYED SINCERE,
SHOWING GROWTH IS STRENGTH, NOT FEAR.
WITH COURAGE STRONG AND VISION WIDE,
HE STOOD FOR TRUTH AND HUMAN RIGHTS.
MALCOLM X REMINDS US ALL,
STAND TALL, SPEAK TRUE, NEVER FALL.

Short Bio

Malcolm X (later known as El Hajj Malik El Shabazz) was a powerful leader who taught Black people to love themselves and stand with dignity. He believed in discipline, education, and truth. His life teaches us to think for ourselves and stand boldly for justice

Lil' Malcolm

QUEEN MOTHER MOORE

QUEEN MOTHER AUDLEY STOOD SO WISE,
WITH STEADY VOICE AND FEARLESS EYES.
SHE SPOKE OF JUSTICE, LAND, AND RIGHT,
AND KEPT THE FLAME OF FREEDOM BRIGHT.
IN SIXTY-EIGHT, HER NAME WAS SIGNED,
FOR SELF-DETERMINATION OF HER KIND.
SHE CALLED HER PEOPLE TO STAND TALL,
SAYING DIGNITY BELONGS TO ALL.
A MOTHER'S STRENGTH, BOTH BOLD AND CLEAR,
SHE TAUGHT US TRUTH, NOT DOUBT OR FEAR.
WITH WISDOM DEEP AND SPIRIT SURE,
SHE WORKED SO FREEDOM WOULD ENDURE.

Short Bio

Your Queen Mother Audley Moore (1898–1997) was a powerful activist known as the "Mother of Reparations." She believed that African descendants in the United States deserved justice, land, and self-determination. In 1968, she became one of the early signers of the Declaration of Independence for the Republic of New Afrika, a movement calling for freedom and nationhood. She encouraged Black women to stand proudly beside Black men in the struggle for liberation. Her wisdom and lifelong dedication inspired generations to continue the work for dignity and repair.

Lil' Queen

GEORGE L. JACKSON

Short Bio

George Lester Jackson (1941–1971) became known for his powerful transformation through education and self-discipline. He believed that knowledge could help people grow beyond their circumstances. His writings encouraged critical thinking, personal development, and commitment to uplifting communities. Today, he is remembered by many as a symbol of transformation through learning and self-awareness.

LIL' GEORGE

IDA B. WELLS

IDA B. WELLS WAS BOLD AND BRIGHT,
SHE USED HER WORDS TO FIGHT FOR RIGHT.
WHEN OTHERS FEARED TO SPEAK OUT LOUD,
SHE STOOD UP STRONG AND MADE US PROUD.
WITH PEN IN HAND AND STEADY HEART,
SHE TORE INJUSTICE ALL APART.
SHE TOLD THE TRUTH SO ALL COULD SEE
THE PAIN BEHIND INEQUALITY.
THEY TRIED TO SILENCE WHAT SHE WROTE,
BUT COURAGE ROSE WITHIN HER THROAT.
SHE TRAVELED FAR, SHE WOULD NOT HIDE,
WITH TRUTH AND JUSTICE AS HER GUIDE.
SHE SHOWED THE WORLD THAT WORDS ARE POWER,
THAT BRAVERY BLOOMS LIKE A FLOWER.
HER VOICE STILL ECHOES, CLEAR AND STRONG —
REMINDING US TO RIGHT WHAT'S WRONG.

Short Bio

Ida B. Wells (1862–1931) was a journalist, educator, and civil rights activist who bravely exposed injustice through her writing. She investigated and reported on the unfair treatment and violence faced by African Americans during her lifetime, even when it was dangerous to do so. Her newspaper work and public speeches helped raise awareness across the country and around the world. Ida B. Wells believed that truth and knowledge could bring change, and her fearless voice continues to inspire people to stand up for justice.

Lil' Ida B.

JOHN BROWN

JOHN BROWN BELIEVED WITH ALL HIS MIGHT,
THAT SLAVERY WAS NOT RIGHT.
HE SAW THE CHAINS, HE HEARD THE CRIES,
AND WOULD NOT TURN AWAY HIS EYES.
HE SAID THAT FREEDOM MUST BE REAL,
NOT JUST WORDS THAT LEADERS FEEL.
HE STOOD UP FIRM WHEN OTHERS FEARED,
AND SPOKE THE TRUTH THAT SOME HAD CLEARED.
HE WORKED WITH FRIENDS BOTH NEAR AND FAR,
WHO DREAMED OF FREEDOM'S SHINING STAR.
HE SHOWED THAT STANDING FOR WHAT'S FAIR
MEANS CHOOSING COURAGE OVER CARE.
HIS LIFE REMINDS US LOUD AND CLEAR,
TO STAND FOR JUSTICE YEAR BY YEAR.

Short Bio

John Brown (1800–1859) was an abolitionist who believed slavery was wrong and worked to end it in the United States. He supported freedom for enslaved people and partnered with others who wanted justice and equality. His strong actions and beliefs made him a controversial figure in history, but many people remember him for his commitment to ending slavery. His story is often told as part of the larger struggle that led to the Civil War and the end of slavery in America.

Lil' John

JAMES BALDWIN

JAMES BALDWIN WROTE WITH FIRE AND GRACE,
TRUTH SHINING BRIGHT UPON EACH PAGE.
HE SAW THE WORLD WITH CAREFUL EYES,
AND SPOKE OF LOVE BENEATH THE LIES.
HIS WORDS WERE SHARP, BUT FULL OF CARE,
HE TOLD HARD TRUTHS BECAUSE HE DARED.
HE WROTE OF PAIN, HE WROTE OF HOPE,
HE TAUGHT OUR HEARTS HOW TO COPE.
FROM HARLEM STREETS TO LANDS AFAR,
HIS VOICE BECAME A GUIDING STAR.
HE SHOWED THAT STORIES HELP US SEE
THE KIND OF WORLD WE WANT TO BE.
WITH COURAGE WRAPPED INSIDE HIS PEN,
HE CHANGED THE MINDS OF WOMEN AND MEN.
HE PROVED THAT TRUTH, THOUGH SOMETIMES HARD,
CAN HEAL THE SOUL AND GUARD THE HEART.

Short Bio

James Baldwin (1924–1987) was a writer, speaker, and civil rights thinker known for his powerful essays and novels. Through his books and speeches, he explored issues of race, identity, justice, and love in America. Baldwin believed that honesty and self-reflection were necessary for growth and healing. His words continue to inspire readers around the world to think deeply, speak truthfully, and care for one another.

LIL' JAMES

BLACK HISTORY 365